# Salmon Migration

by Grace Hansen

**abdopublishing.com**

Published by Abdo Kids, a division of ABDO, P.O. Box 398166, Minneapolis, Minnesota 55439.



Printed in the United States of America, North Mankato, Minnesota.

052017

092017

Photo Credits: iStock, Minden Pictures, Shutterstock

Production Contributors: Teddy Borth, Jennie Forsberg, Grace Hansen

Design Contributors: Dorothy Toth, Laura Mitchell

Publisher's Cataloging in Publication Data

Names: Hansen, Grace, author.

Title: Salmon migration / by Grace Hansen.

Description: Minneapolis, Minnesota : Abdo Kids, 2018 | Series: Animal migration | Includes bibliographical references and index.

Identifiers: LCCN 2016962370 | ISBN 9781532100314 (lib. bdg.) | ISBN 9781532101007 (ebook) | ISBN 9781532101557 (Read-to-me ebook)

Subjects: LCSH: Salmon--Juvenile literature. | Salmon migration--Juvenile literature.

Classification: DDC 597.5--dc23

LC record available at http://lccn.loc.gov/2016962370

# Table of Contents

## Salmon

Wild salmon can be found in the Atlantic and Pacific oceans. There are five main Pacific Salmon **species**. They are Chinook, chum, coho, pink, and sockeye.

Chinook

chum

coho

pink

sockeye

## To the Ocean!

All salmon **species** are born in rivers and streams. Chinook and pink salmon swim to the ocean when they are **fingerlings**. Other species wait one to three years before going to the ocean.

Once in the ocean, certain **species** travel farther than others. Pink salmon stay fairly close to the **mouth** of their river home.

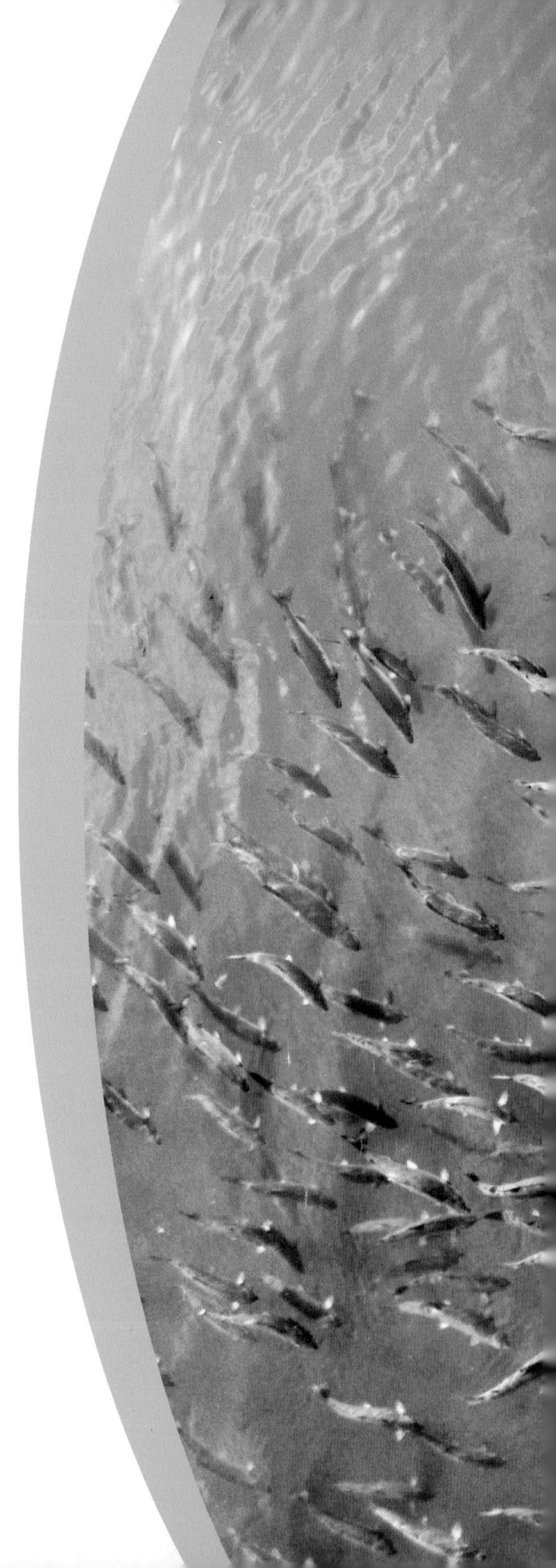

Sockeye and Chinook salmon swim farther into the ocean. They may swim more than 2,600 miles (4184.3 km) from their river home.

At some point, all salmon travel home. Chinook will stay out at sea for as long as six years. Sockeye salmon swim home after one to four years.

## Swimming Upstream

Salmon return to the same river or stream they were born in. This usually happens in the fall. The swim upstream is a difficult one. Hungry bears can be waiting!

The salmon that make it home have changed color. Sockeye and coho salmon turn bright red. This means they are ready to **spawn**.

Females dig small holes in the **riverbed**. They lay eggs in the holes. Males **fertilize** the eggs. Females cover the eggs.

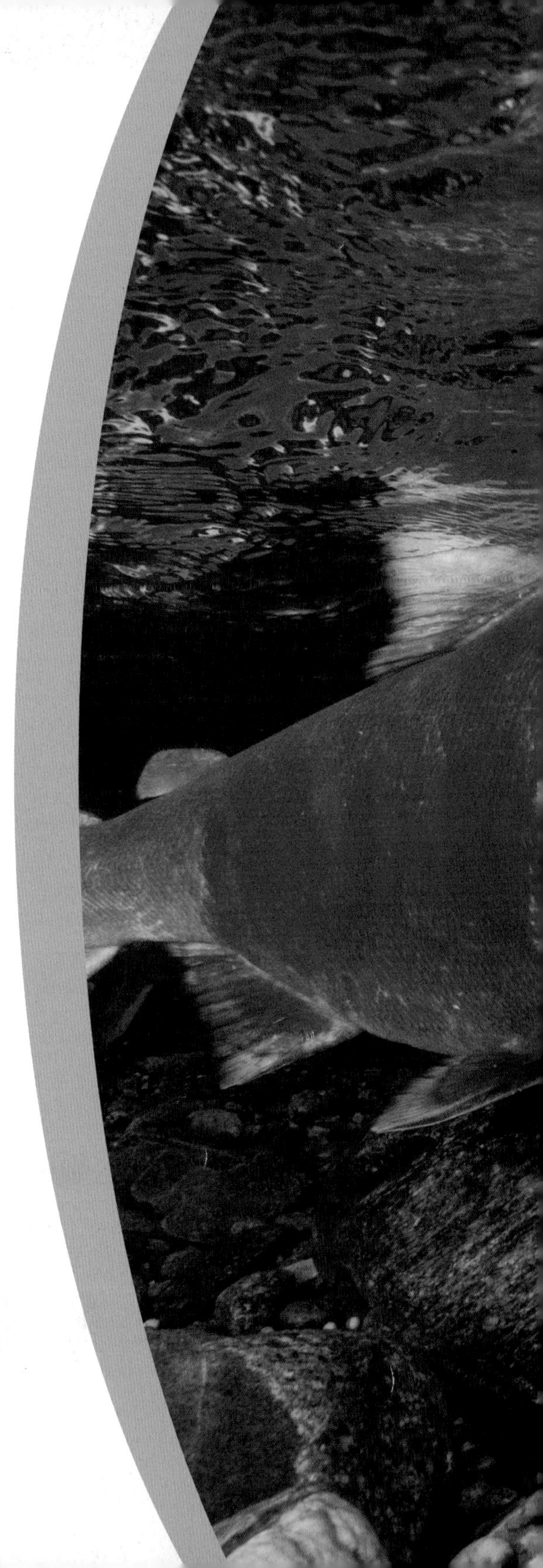

Most salmon die after they spawn. But many new salmon are born! They will swim to the ocean and return like their parents did. The cycle will begin again.

# Salmon Migration Routes

pink coho Chinook chum sockeye

# Glossary

**fertilize** – to make an egg able to grow and develop.

**fingerling** – a young or small salmon.

**mouth** – the point where a river meets an ocean or a lake.

**riverbed** – the ground at the bottom of a river.

**spawn** – to produce young especially in large numbers.

**species** – a group of animals that look alike, share many characteristics, and can produce young together.

# Index



# abdokids.com

Use this code to log on to abdokids.com and access crafts, games, videos and more!